ANIMAL
INSTINCTS

PAIRED:

Two outsiders who have a way with animals.
Cesar Millan was an immigrant from Mexico with
no money to his name. Then he became the world-
famous "Dog Whisperer." Temple Grandin learned
to cope with autism and use her gifts to ease
the suffering of millions of animals.

"One of the things I love most about America
is that it is a place of many options. I am
grateful for all these choices. I want my readers
to know that there are so many possibilities,
they are sure to find something that works
for them and their dogs."

Cesar Millan

"Animals taught me the meaning of life.
[When I saw cows slaughtered,] I felt so
deeply that we had to give them a decent life
and a painless death. But I also thought,
'When it gets to be my time, will I have
accomplished something of ultimate value?'"

Temple Grandin

Photographs © 2012: Alamy Images: 43 (Angela Hampton Picture Library), 14 (J. Hutfluss/
Tierfotoagentur), cover (Gabriele Maerz); AP Images/Rob Loud/PictureGroup: 97; Corbis Images:
56 (Lowell Georgia), 62 (Chuck Haney/AgStock Images), 78 (Helen King); Getty Images: back
cover right, 3 right (Vera Anderson/WireImage), back cover left, 3 left (Neilson Barnard), 28
(John Chapple), 12 (Gregg DeGuire/WireImage), 52 (Dr. Billy Ingram/WireImage), 20 (Jeffrey
L. Jaquish/ZingPix.com), 49 (Menahem Kahana/AFP), 39 (Riccardo S. Savi); iStockphoto/Jean
Frooms: 42; Kobal Collection/Picture Desk/Van Redin/HBO: 95; Matthew B. Slaby/Luceo Images:
54, 92, 99; Media Bakery: 17, 44, 45; National Geographic Stock/Mark Thiessen: 51; NEWSCOM:
34 (Jeff Grace/La Opinon Photos), 10 (Paul Harris), 46 (Nancy Kaszerman/ZUME Press); Redux
Pictures/Monica Almeida/The New York Times: 36; Rosalie Winard: 80, 100; Temple Grandin,
Ph.D: 64, 70, 74, 82, 86; The Image Works/David Grossman: 73; The Orange County Register/
Cindy Yamanaka/www.ocregister.com: 25; USDA/Scott Bauer: 89.

Library of Congress Cataloging-in-Publication Data

Maher, Jack, 1966-
Animal instincts / Jack Maher.
p. cm. -- (On the record)
Includes bibliographical references and index.
ISBN-13: 978-0-531-22560-8 (pbk.)
ISBN-10: 0-531-22560-7
1. Millan, Cesar--Juvenile literature. 2. Grandin, Temple--Juvenile
literature. 3. Animal specialists--United States--Biography--Juvenile
literature. 4. Women animal specialists--United
States--Biography--Juvenile literature. 5. Pets--Behavior. 6.
Livestock--Behavior. I. Title.
SF31.M34 2012
636.08'3092273--dc22
[B]
2011015896

Tod Olson, Series Editor
Marie O'Neill, Creative Director
Curriculum Concepts International, Production
Thanks to John DiConsiglio

14 15 16   40   21

ANIMAL INSTINCTS

Some people *really* have a way with animals.

Jack Maher

Contents

ALPHA DOG

Cesar Millan came to the U.S. with almost
nothing to his name. Now he's the pack
leader of a dog-training empire.
From rottweilers to pit bulls, the
"Dog Whisperer" has the magic touch
with problem pets.

Millan poses with his best friend and right-hand dog, Daddy, on the red carpet at an awards show. Daddy, who died at 16 in 2010, was a calm, sweet dog who helped to change misconceptions about pit bulls.

1
Saving Scarlett

Scarlett weighed just a few pounds when her family brought her home. She had a pair of adorable "bat ears." The French bulldog looked more cuddly than vicious. But soon the house became a battleground.

It was a pet-heavy household already. There was a wide variety of dogs and a pet rabbit. Small, black-and-white Scarlett was the newest addition. At first everything went smoothly.

French bulldogs are muscular dogs that can weigh up to 30 pounds. They need firm training and love from their owners.

Then disaster struck. The rabbit escaped from its cage. It attracted the attention of young Scarlett. She attacked. The rabbit was rescued but lost an eye in the fight.

Shocked and dismayed, the family contacted Cesar Millan. It was 2005, and Millan was the new authority on problem dogs. Millan met with Scarlett and the gang. Then he gave his advice for dealing with her aggression.

Be calm and assertive, Millan tells dog owners. Stand straight with your shoulders squared. Don't look the dog in the eye. And show it who's in control.

Scarlett didn't get the message. A few weeks later she bit the leg off a Chihuahua. For the family, it was the last straw. They sent Scarlett to Millan's Dog Psychology

Center in Los Angeles. That's where Millan helps the most difficult dogs.

At the center, Millan teaches troubled dogs like Scarlett who's boss. That's a lesson many dogs in the United States never learn, says Millan. He came to the U.S. from Mexico in 1990. Since then he's observed that many American dogs are treated like spoiled children. Their owners smother them with affection and rarely discipline them. "Here in America, the dogs take over," Millan says.

And that doesn't make for happy dogs. In Millan's view, dogs don't want to be human. They want to be dogs. They crave leadership and discipline.

In Scarlett's case, her owners' home had very little order. There were few rules, and the family was often out. Millan thought

Millan was shocked to see that dogs in the U.S. are often treated to birthday parties, stylish wardrobes, and even diamond-studded collars. And as many as 40 percent of American dogs are overweight.

he knew why Scarlett was aggressive. Her owners had not worked with her enough. "There was no balance in the pack," Millan says. "So Scarlett ended up acting out. Then she got blamed for her 'bad' behavior."

Scarlett quickly responded to Millan's training. Millan insists he doesn't pick favorites. But he admits he's very attached to her. "She's so sweet and calm she can go anywhere with me. I think of her as my good-luck charm. Whenever I need an extra stroke of luck, I rub her tummy. She's never failed me yet." Millan even brings Scarlett to work. She helps him train other dogs.

Scarlett's case is a perfect example of Millan's most famous saying: "I train people and rehabilitate dogs." Working with difficult dogs like Scarlett doesn't usually come naturally. Owners need to be taught how to raise a calm, obedient dog. And Scarlett needed a knowledgeable trainer like Millan to achieve her full potential.

That message has taken Millan on an amazing journey. He's become the top dog in a $90 million media empire.

A sheepdog rounds up a flock of sheep. When Millan was growing up, he watched his grandfather train dogs to herd farm animals.

2
The Dog Boy

Growing up in Mexico, Cesar Millan had a nickname—*El Perrero*, the Dog Boy. He hung out with other kids. But his heart wasn't in it. He longed to be running with the dogs on his grandfather's farm.

When he was young, Millan made the hour-long trip to the farm on weekends and vacations whenever he could. His grandfather raised goats, chickens, and pigs. Cesar liked to run through the hills with packs of wild dogs. He watched with fascination as his grandfather trained mangy mutts to round up cattle and sheep. Cesar studied the dogs' behavior until he felt he understood them as well as he understood himself.

The farmhouse had just four rooms and no running water. But to Cesar it was paradise. His grandfather taught him generations of dog-training secrets. Never work against Mother Nature, he told the boy. Dogs are dogs. Don't treat them like people.

"To him, everything about a dog was beautiful," Millan later recalled. "He didn't love animals in the way Americans love animals. He would get a kick out of that— to see a birthday party for a dog . . . He was the epitome of honesty, integrity, loyalty. And that's what he loved about animals."

Most important, Cesar's grandfather taught him that dogs are members of a pack-oriented species. That includes all dogs—from farm hounds to the most pampered poodles. Some dog owners treat their pets as companions. But Cesar's grandfather insisted that dogs are followers at heart. They are happier with a firm pack leader than with an owner who spoils them.

When Cesar was about seven, he and his parents moved to the city of Mazatlán. Cesar hated the cramped streets of the city. He rarely got to visit his grandfather's farm. "I was indoors all the time," he said. "I had no friends but dogs."

Cesar spent hours on his apartment couch, flipping through TV reruns. But he bolted to attention when he came across old black-and-white shows starring animal heroes like Rin Tin Tin and Lassie. He loved to watch Lassie rescue kids from abandoned wells and freezing cold ponds.

Suddenly Cesar knew what he wanted to do with his life. Walking through Mazatlán with his mother one day, he stopped in front of a statue. He vowed to his mother that someday he'd go to Hollywood and become the world's greatest dog trainer. He knew he had the skill to train dogs just like the ones he'd seen on TV.

Millan's parents were too poor to send him to the United States. But in 1990, when Millan was 21, his family managed to scrape together $100. He said his good-byes and left for Tijuana, a city on the U.S. border.

A U.S. Border Patrol vehicle drives along the border between Tijuana, Mexico, and San Diego, California. Millan managed to slip across the border on his fourth attempt.

In Tijuana he spent two weeks at a friend's apartment, studying the border. He made three attempts to cross and failed each time.

Finally Millan hired a smuggler known as a coyote to get him over the border. The coyote cost him exactly $100.

Millan set off with the coyote for one final attempt. They approached the border until they saw the lights of border patrol guards. Millan and the coyote hid in a rain-filled ditch. They waited all night, neck-deep in water, for the guards to leave.

Millan was so close to his dream. "It's unbelievable, but not one drop of fear came to me. I was not afraid whatsoever," he later recalled. He simply told himself: "This is what I need to do."

At last the coast was clear. The coyote signaled for Millan to make a dash for the border. Millan ran across a muddy field, through a junkyard, and over a highway into the United States. Drenched and exhausted, he waved down a taxi driver and got a ride to San Diego.

Millan was 21 years old. He spoke no English and knew no one in this new country. He had no place to live. He would have to make it on the streets by himself.

Millan takes a group of dogs out for a run in the streets of Los Angeles. He says that exercise is the key to relaxed and happy dogs.

3
Up from Poverty

Millan lived on San Diego's streets for nearly two months. In tattered clothes, he imagined he looked as ragged as his grandfather's dogs. He knew just one sentence in English: "Do you have application for work?"

Millan never thought of himself as an illegal immigrant. "I felt like a tourist, not an illegal guy running from anything," he recalled. "No place to live, no money. But I never begged."

He survived on hot dogs and free soda refills from convenience stores. Somehow he managed to remain cheerful. "My mom did not allow us to drink soda," he said. "And here, you get refills! For $1.69, you can get all the soda you want!"

Eventually Millan stumbled across a dog-grooming center run by two women. When he walked in, the owners were struggling with an unruly spaniel. Millan calmed the high-strung dog. Then he told the groomers his secret. Their nervous energy was making the dog anxious. Millan approached the spaniel calmly and firmly. It responded by sitting quietly for a haircut.

The owners were so impressed that they offered Millan a job on the spot. Soon he was handling their toughest canine clients and sleeping on a cot in their back room. "I couldn't believe it!" he said. "I bought jeans and a shirt. I'd been wearing the same shirt for two months."

But Millan was still determined to make a name for himself in the movie industry. He said good-bye to the dog groomers and moved to Los Angeles. There he took a job washing limousines. "I was a good car wash guy," he said. "I could clean 13 limousines a day . . . I didn't care what I was doing. If I was a kennel guy or a guy washing cars, I wanted to be the best."

He also tried to get work training dogs. He went door to door, offering his services. Embarrassed by his poor English, he usually didn't charge more than $10 a session. "My goods were good, but my delivery wasn't," he says.

Soon Millan opened his first pet training center. His office was a white Chevy Astro van. But he didn't care. Working with dogs lifted his spirits. "I couldn't just be around people," he said. "I'm used to being around dogs. The pack teaches me every day. They know when I'm down. They keep me grounded."

Millan became a familiar sight in Los Angeles. Heads turned to watch the stocky man whiz through the streets on in-line skates. Behind him trailed a pack of leashed dogs. "I'd take out 30 dogs, all walking behind me. People would stop and stare as I'd go through Beverly Hills with rottweilers and pit bulls," he recalls. "I'd take them for four-hour walks and charge $10. Their owners were amazed when I'd bring back calm, contented dogs."

By 1995, Millan had fallen in love with a Mexican American woman named Ilusion. They were married and had a son. But they were having trouble making ends meet. "We couldn't even afford Pampers," Millan remembers.

Around this time, Millan finally got his first big break. Actress Jada Pinkett Smith (then Jada Pinkett) asked for his help. She couldn't control her rottweilers. Millan impressed the actress by taming her dogs. She started recommending him to her friends in the movie business.

Millan eventually shared his dream with Pinkett Smith. He wanted to be the next Lassie trainer, maybe even star in his own TV show. She agreed that his skills were amazing. But his English was poor. She

Millan opened the Dog Psychology Center in Los Angeles in 1998. There he rehabilitated troubled dogs. Eventually Millan was able to move the center to a rural area where the dogs have more space.

hired a tutor for him, and Millan worked hard to master the language.

In 1998 Millan opened the Dog Psychology Center in South Central L.A. He boarded dogs at the center for as long as it took to get them under control. His daily walks were the key to his training. They were also his best form of advertising. "People would see me with my pack. They'd think, if that guy can control 30 dogs, he can help me with mine," Millan says.

Before long Millan was handling dogs for stars like Oprah Winfrey. When a 2002 newspaper article publicized his talents, the National Geographic Channel came calling—and offered him his own TV show.

Millan walks a shar-pei mix named Chase for an episode of *Dog Whisperer with Cesar Millan* in 2009. Chase had aggression problems and kept attacking his own reflection in the mirror.

Who would have thought that a TV show about dog training would become a smash hit? Millan's show, *Dog Whisperer with Cesar Millan*, began in 2004. And soon it had millions of fans.

Millan says he has one secret. The dogs are never the real problem. It's their two-legged owners who cause the most damage.

According to Millan, dogs have three primary needs. They have to have exercise, discipline, and affection—in that order.

Too often, dog owners overdo the affection and ignore the other two needs. Millan urges owners not to give dogs affection when they are fearful, anxious, or excited. That just encourages them to behave badly.

On his TV show, Millan tries to help unruly dogs and "train" their owners. In each episode he arrives at a home where a pet has taken over. With what he calls "calm, assertive energy," Millan restores order.

Millan has a commanding presence with dogs. Every dog, he says, carefully watches body language. It tries to decide who is a pack leader and who is a pushover. Millan leaves no doubt about the answer. He stands straight, with his shoulders squared. He breathes evenly and never

Millan faces down a dog named Doc. Millan squares his
shoulders and stands up straight. This shows Doc that
Millan is the pack leader.

looks a dog in the eye. Eye contact can be a trigger for a dog to attack.

Millan isn't shy about using his hands to show dogs who's the boss. He might jab or pinch them on the neck or shoulder. That imitates a nip from a pack leader. He sometimes pins dogs to the ground. Or he might give them a sharp smack on the head.

Not everyone agrees with Millan's methods. The American Humane Association has called them "inhumane and inappropriate." Plenty of dog trainers also criticize Millan. They argue that dogs should be treated as companions—not as followers. These trainers say they can train difficult dogs with treats and rewards instead of punishment.

Millan reminds his critics that he often deals with the most extreme cases. He helps violent dogs that are one step away from being put down. "People come to me with dogs that have almost killed them," he says. "They're seriously dangerous dogs."

Millan also insists that a submissive dog is a happy dog. The battling pit bulls, unruly spaniels, and headstrong rottweilers don't really want to be pack leaders. Everyone is happier, he says, when humans take charge.

Most dogs don't bite the hands that feed them. But that doesn't mean they are happy or well behaved. Some dogs beg for food at the dinner table. Others lead their owners on walks instead of the other way around. Some bring toys and insist on a game of fetch. Or they lean on their owners and demand to be petted. According to Millan, these are all signs that the dog thinks it's the boss.

Here are a few tips the Dog Whisperer might offer to the owners of difficult dogs.

Doggie Workouts

Dogs need exercise to burn off energy. Most dogs spend 22 hours a day inside. That can make them restless and tense.

Dogs need exercise!

Letting your dog out in the backyard doesn't count. "The backyard is not exercise," Millan says. "It doesn't represent freedom. It doesn't represent fun."

Long walks keep dogs in a calm state of mind, Millan says. He leads his pack on early morning runs in the mountains. What if that's never going to happen at your house? Millan recommends walking your dog at least 45 minutes a day.

Walk This Way

When you take your dog for a walk, always keep in mind that you're the pack leader. Never let your dog walk in front of you. Make sure it walks beside or behind you. That communicates that you're in charge.

This well-trained pit bull doesn't strain the leash.

If you want your dog to stop, just stop. Don't bark orders. An occasional quick tug on the leash will help you guide your pet. Eventually it should learn to follow you even if you drop the leash.

Setting Limits

You're the boss. But that doesn't mean you have to be tough all the time. According to Millan, there's nothing

No begging!

wrong with offering your dog scraps from the dinner table— as long as you've finished eating first. "Pack leaders do share food with followers. But they wait until the pack leader is finished," Millan says.

Did he ask permission?

Likewise, it's okay for your dog to sleep in your bed. But it shouldn't be allowed to jump up on its own. "When a dog invites himself, that's when [he claims] the bed," Millan explains. "But if you make him wait . . . he goes into a calm, submissive state. Then it's okay to invite the dog in."

Millan promotes the release of his TV show on DVD.
Fans brought their dogs to a bookstore in New York
City to meet the star.

5
Cesar's Empire

In just over a decade, Cesar Millan fulfilled his promise to himself. He has become the most famous dog trainer in the U.S.—and probably in the world. At its height, *Dog Whisperer with Cesar Millan* drew nearly 11 million viewers.

The TV show was only the beginning of his multimillion-dollar business. Millan has written five best-selling books. He publishes a monthly magazine called *Cesar's Way*. His website gets more than 400,000 hits a month. Every year he sells millions of dollars' worth of DVDs, books, and pet supplies. He built a new 43-acre Dog Psychology Center in California's Santa Clarita Mountains. It's a haven for troubled pets. Millan calls it "Disneyland for dogs." His $10 days are behind him. Millan charges between $10,000 and $100,000 for a private session.

But the Dog Whisperer doesn't devote all his time to celebrity pets. He runs a foundation for abused dogs. True, he also oversees a media empire and a pack of 50 troubled dogs. But he says success hasn't turned him into a fat cat. "I'm the same guy who jumped the border," he insists. "I just have different clothes."

Millan often returns to Mexico to visit his family. He takes his mother to

Abandoned dogs wander through New Orleans after
it was hit by Hurricane Katrina in 2005. Millan took in
three New Orleans dogs at his Dog Psychology Center.

the statue in Mazatlán where he once vowed to become the world's greatest dog trainer. Over shrimp tacos, they marvel at their good fortune. How did a penniless guy become a global TV star? Millan says he's grateful for the opportunities he's found in the United States. He is determined to repay the world for his good fortune by helping owners and their pets live together peacefully.

"Peace, relaxation, trust, respect," Millan says. "That is my goal."

Millan plays fetch at his Dog Psychology Center. "If I were a tree," he writes in one book, "all the wonderful people in my life would be the ones who influenced my growth, but dogs would still be my roots."

Cesar Millan signs copies of his book *Cesar's Rules: Your Way to Train a Well-Behaved Dog.* His books on dog training have sold millions of copies.

Cesar Millan

Born August 27, 1969; grew up in Culiacán and Mazatlán, Mexico

Current home:

Became a U.S. citizen in 2009 and lives in California

Life's work:

Rehabilitating dogs; training people

Day job:

Professional dog trainer, writer, and TV star

Website:

www.cesarsway.com

Author of:

Be the Pack Leader: Use Cesar's Way to Transform Your Dog . . . and Your Life

Cesar's Rules: Your Way to Train a Well-Behaved Dog

Cesar's Way: The Natural, Everyday Guide to Understanding and Correcting Common Dog Problems

How to Raise the Perfect Dog: Through Puppyhood and Beyond

A Member of the Family: The Ultimate Guide to Living with a Happy, Healthy Dog

Star of:

Dog Whisperer with Cesar Millan

He says:

"Discipline isn't about showing a dog who's boss. It's about taking responsibility for a living creature you have brought into your world."

BREAKING THROUGH

As an autistic child, Temple Grandin struggled to communicate with the rest of the world. Now she uses her special talents to teach people how to treat cattle and other livestock humanely.

Temple Grandin was shocked by the chaos of her aunt's farm. The farm animals, she noticed, seemed to have a similar reaction.

6

A Cow's-Eye View

Temple Grandin opened the wooden gate to her aunt's farm. Instantly she was under attack. She wasn't gored by a bull or bitten by an angry pig. She was attacked by sights and sounds. The Arizona heat seemed to slash across her skin. Dogs were barking, farmhands were hollering, cows were mooing. Every sound swirled louder and louder around her head.

It was the early 1960s, and Temple was in high school at the time. She lived in Boston but was spending the summer at her aunt Ann Brecheen's cattle ranch in Tempe, Arizona. Temple's mother, Eustacia Cutler, was hoping the change would be good for her daughter.

Temple had been born with autism, a neurological condition that affects as many as a million and a half Americans. (*Neurological* means "having to do with the nervous system.") Many people with autism feel overwhelmed by sights, sounds, and physical sensations. Some might have trouble relating to people socially. And they may struggle with speech and conversation.

When Temple was growing up, ordinary experiences could send her into panic attacks. School bells cut like a dentist's drill through her brain. A dress rustling against her legs scratched like sandpaper.

She couldn't stand to be held or touched. Even when she was a toddler, an embrace from her mother felt like a straightjacket.

"When people hugged me, I just got an overwhelming tidal wave of stimuli just going over me. I couldn't tolerate it, so I'd pull away," she said. "I wanted to be hugged. I wanted to feel the nice feeling. But it was just too overwhelming. I couldn't stand it."

To find some comfort, Temple would wrap herself in blankets and crawl under sofa cushions. But as a teenager she grew more and more anxious. Nothing seemed to calm her when she started to panic. Temple's mother didn't know what else to do. So she sent Temple to Aunt Ann Brecheen's cattle farm.

At first the farm was no more relaxing than Temple's home in Boston. There were so many noises. The roosters crowed. The frightened chickens squawked. The sounds were as upsetting as those in the city.

But Temple loved the cows. She spent hours watching them circle the tight corral. They reminded her of herself. Every loud noise made them skittish. They reacted each time a tool made a sound or a gate slammed.

One afternoon, Temple watched the cowboys herd cattle into a rectangular pen known as a "squeeze chute." Squeeze chutes are cagelike devices with moveable walls made of wood or metal. They're used to hold cattle while the animals are being vaccinated or branded.

Temple was fascinated. The restless cattle seemed to calm down as soon as the walls pressed against their hides. It was like . . . a hug. The squeeze chute brought relief to an anxious cow, she thought. Maybe it could also work for her.

Temple asked her aunt to put her in the squeeze chute. It was a crazy idea, and Aunt Ann couldn't imagine it. But Temple talked her into helping.

Temple crawled into the chute. Her aunt pulled a lever and the walls slowly pressed against Temple's body. She fought a surge of panic. Then she felt a soothing rush.

The chute's pressure felt like a hug. But it wasn't disturbing, the way human hugs were. It quieted the screeching in her brain. "This was the first time I ever

A ranch hand vaccinates cattle in a squeeze chute.
The chute holds the cows still and calms them.

felt really comfortable in my own skin," Grandin later wrote.

Neither Temple nor her aunt could have known what was happening as Temple knelt in the cattle chute. The teenager was on her way to important insights into the treatment of animals and the nature of autism. Her remarkable story was about to begin.

Temple Grandin kneels between the walls of a squeeze chute. She had watched how cattle were calmed by the firm, steady pressure of the chute, and she found that it calmed her as well.

7
Learning Experience

The moment of peace in the cattle chute was a rare experience for Temple. Before that summer, her life had been anything but peaceful.

Temple Grandin was born in 1947. She began to show signs of autism when she was just six months old. As a toddler, she hated to be held. She'd stiffen up and pull away from her mother's embrace. She clawed at anyone who tried to touch her. She even threw her own feces when she couldn't control her rage. And by age three, Temple hadn't uttered a word.

When Temple was still young, a doctor gave her mother grim news. Temple would probably never be able to speak or function in society. He suggested that Temple spend the rest of her life in an institution.

Even today, experts don't fully understand autism. No one is sure what causes it, and no one has found a cure. It seems that autism affects the parts of the brain that control language and social relationships. Autism also limits abstract thought. That's the ability to understand concepts as opposed to concrete facts.

Many kids with autism display symptoms like Temple's. They may have trouble learning to speak. Loud noises and contact with other people can be terribly upsetting.

Too much noise or activity can send a child with autism into a raging tantrum.

When Temple was diagnosed, there were few strategies for helping autistic children. Parents were frequently told that there was nothing that could be done. Many kids were sent to institutions for people with mental illnesses. Others withdrew into an isolated world within their own heads. They were separated from everyday human experiences and emotions.

But Temple's mother refused to send her daughter away. Instead she worked hard to help Temple adjust to her condition and to the world around her. She read to Temple for hours and found her a speech therapist. By the age of four, Temple began to speak. Her parents hired a caregiver who would spend hours playing games with her. Temple loved board games like Chinese Checkers and Parcheesi. "They kept me occupied so I couldn't tune out," Grandin recalled.

The family exposed Temple to as many childhood experiences as possible. They sent her to summer camp. They found small private schools to work with her. Today Grandin credits her mother's efforts with helping her learn to operate in society. "Everyone worked hard to make sure that I was engaged," she said. "They knew I was different but not *less*."

Still, daily life was a challenge for Temple. She could go into a panic at any moment. A school bell could set her off. So could the ringing of a telephone. "I was scared to go into certain rooms [at school] because I didn't know when the bell was going to go off," she recalled. "The school bell—that hurt my ears . . . I sometimes screamed [and] flung myself on the floor."

After eighth grade, Temple left her small private school for a much larger school. She got less personal attention there, and she was miserable. Students teased her. They called her "tape recorder" because she repeated phrases again and again.

Temple felt angry and cornered, and she lashed out. After biting a teacher's leg and throwing a book at a classmate, she was expelled.

Temple's mother had always wanted to keep her daughter in school with mainstream kids. But she finally decided it was time for a change. She sent Temple to the Hampshire Country School. That's a

At Hampshire Country School, Temple enjoyed caring for the school's horses. "I got work experience taking care of horses," Grandin says. "A lot of quirky kids get into problems not getting work experience."

boarding school for gifted kids who have trouble getting along socially.

Temple thrived in her new environment. The teachers understood her needs. And they saw how bright she was. Temple couldn't grasp abstract subjects like English literature and foreign languages. But she excelled in science. At Hampshire Country, Temple met William Carlock. He was a science teacher who became her mentor. Carlock encouraged Temple to take on new challenges, like building model rockets for the school rocket club.

Hampshire Country also offered Temple a chance to work with the school's horses. She spent a lot of time at the stables and observed that the animals were extremely sensitive, just like her. Sudden, jerky motions made them skittish. But firm touches and steady pressure calmed them. They seemed to like the feel of her palm gently pressing against their sides.

But even in the supportive environment of Hampshire Country, Temple's anxiety grew. Her panic attacks became even more frequent.

Temple's mother suggested a summer vacation on Aunt Ann's Arizona farm. The change of scenery might be worth a try.

A child with special needs receives hippotherapy—therapy done on horseback. Many believe that hippotherapy can help with a range of conditions, including autism, by improving a patient's coordination, speech, and emotional well-being. "People and animals are supposed to be together," Grandin writes.

A young Grandin works on a project. She says: "You get the visual thinkers like me that are good at art, good at things like industrial designs and graphics, but have problems with math … because it's not visual."

8
Squeeze Machine

Throughout the summer on her aunt's ranch, Temple thought about the experience she'd had in the cattle chute. Steady pressure calmed her—just the way it soothed cows and horses. She began to recognize an important connection between her own autism and the behavior of these animals. That realization, she said later, "was the best thing that ever happened to me."

When she returned to school, Temple built her own squeeze machine with plywood and an air compressor. The compressor squeezed the wooden walls together until they delivered a soothing hug. She found that just 15 minutes in the machine produced a calming effect that lasted for hours.

In 1966 Grandin enrolled at Franklin Pierce College. (It is now Franklin Pierce University.) She brought her squeeze machine with her. College officials did not appreciate the genius of the device. Grandin's roommates freaked out at the sight of her kneeling between two large wooden boards. The school ordered Grandin to dismantle the machine. They even sent workers to haul it to a dumpster.

Grandin explained the purpose of the squeeze machine. But she had trouble convincing people that it actually worked. William Carlock, her high school science teacher, suggested an experiment. Grandin asked other students to crawl into the squeeze machine. Then she recorded their reactions. Most of them found the machine relaxing.

In 1970 Grandin graduated from Franklin Pierce with a degree in psychology. She got a job in the cattle industry. As she studied for her master's degree, she often toured slaughterhouses.

Grandin wasn't naive. She knew the cows were marked for death. They had been bred to become food. Besides, she says, "When an animal dies in a well-run slaughter plant, that's much more peaceful than out in nature . . . If I [were] an

The United States slaughters about 35 million cattle a year for food. Conditions in slaughterhouses are often brutal. Grandin's goal is to make livestock suffer less before they die.

animal, I'd rather go to a slaughter plant than have my guts dined on [by a predator] while I was still alive."

But most of the slaughterhouses Grandin saw were not well run. Cattle were prodded with electric shocks and packed into dirty pens. Cows tripped on metal slopes. They broke their legs and dragged others down with them. Some of them drowned while stumbling through a pesticide wash known as a dip vat.

Grandin saw cows get spooked by sudden movements. They'd panic as they were led to slaughter. And the deafening noise overloaded Grandin's senses. Every slaughterhouse rang with shouting workers, clanging metal machinery, and the bellowing of terrified cows.

Grandin says, "I do come from the perspective that using animals for food or agriculture or pets is acceptable, but we have got to give those animals a good life. Whether it is cattle or dogs we have got to give them a good life."

"We raise these animals. We must give them a decent life," Grandin later reflected. "I think that's extremely important. They feel pain. They feel fear."

The cattle were going to die. That was a fact. But their deaths could be humane. "When I see people abuse cattle, it makes me very angry," she says. "And I want to change things."

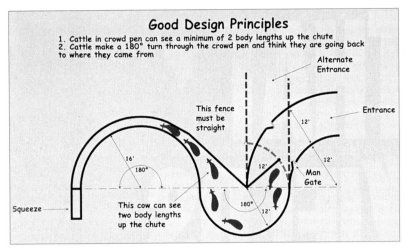

Good Design Principles

1. Cattle in crowd pen can see a minimum of 2 body lengths up the chute
2. Cattle make a 180° turn through the crowd pen and think they are going back to where they came from

Alternate Entrance

Entrance

This fence must be straight

16'
180°

12'

12'

12'

Man Gate

Squeeze

This cow can see two body lengths up the chute

180°

12'

Grandin designed this chute to lead cows out of a pen.
The winding path keeps the cows calm.

9

Picturing a
Humane Life

In the gruesome killing rooms of slaughterhouses, Temple Grandin discovered her life's work. She went on to get a master's degree and eventually a PhD in animal science. And she has used her unusual skills to redesign the way Americans get their beef.

According to Grandin, her autism helps her understand the minds of cattle. She describes herself as a "visual thinker." Most people think in words and concepts, she says. When they hear the word "shoe," for example, they're likely to imagine a general idea of what shoes are. But when Grandin hears "shoe," her brain races through images of every shoe she can recall. Boots, loafers, sneakers, and sandals all flash before her eyes in rapid succession. She compares her mind to Google Images—a search engine for pictures.

Like Grandin, farm animals rely on visual clues to manage their environments. "Animals don't think in language," she says. "They think in pictures." A cow may be disturbed by anything from a flash of light to a vivid image from its memory.

Animals can have particularly strong responses to what Grandin calls "fear memories." A horse that was abused by a person with a black hat will remember the event for a long time. But the horse might be afraid of black hats rather than the abusive person. "They make an association, either of sight or sound," Grandin says. She adds that she understands that kind of panic response all too well. "An autistic kid, he can get afraid of seeing a little red fire alarm box." That's because he never knows when "that horrible thing" could go off.

Not all experts agree with the connections Grandin makes between animals and people with autism. Autism affects different people in different ways. Some may have especially visual minds like Grandin. But her critics say it's impossible to generalize about the way all autistic people think.

But that criticism hasn't stopped Grandin. Her goal was to create equipment that

Cows are led through a curved chute designed by Temple Grandin. According to her website, "cattle move through curved [chutes] more easily because they have a natural tendency to go back to where they came from."

lessened the anxiety of cows as they moved through the slaughterhouse. She did the design work without blueprints or notes. She could visualize every detail of the complex new machinery in her head.

Grandin's first breakthrough was a chute designed to lead cattle to slaughter in a curved pattern. Standard chutes directed cows in a straight line. That meant they had a clear view of everything that lay ahead. Say a cow spotted something unexpected in its path—like a steep hill, a plastic bottle, even a spot of sunlight. That could be enough to stop the cow in its tracks. The entire column of cows would come to a halt. The cows could panic, thrash around in the crowded chute, and injure each other.

Grandin based her plans on close observation of cattle behavior. She noticed that cows did not like to move from bright sunlight into a darkened room. Ramps with high walls helped ease the transition.

Grandin also knew from experience how sensitive cows are to noise. "I've worked on getting people to keep their mouths shut when they're moving cattle," she says. She even convinced slaughterhouse managers to repaint their plants. Why? She discovered that cows seem to be disturbed by the color yellow.

It wasn't always easy for Grandin to talk her clients into changing their ways. Her ideas didn't just challenge conventional cow-handling methods. They often seemed absurd. How could cows have a color preference?

A cow swims through a pesticide dip. Grandin designed
a grooved, concrete ramp into the dip vat that cattle
can descend safely. Before Grandin's design, cattle
often slipped on slick metal ramps and were injured
or drowned.

Besides, Grandin was as unconventional as her ideas. Like many people with autism, her social skills were poorly developed. She was blunt with her criticism and spoke in a near-shouting voice. She often wore the same dirty overalls day after day. One employer demanded she use deodorant and change her shirt daily.

Ranchers were often hostile to Grandin. She thinks this was partly because she was a woman working in a mostly male industry. Workers at one ranch covered her car with bloody bull testicles. Grandin took a practical attitude toward the abuse. "As long as they let me work with cows in the feed yard, I didn't mind if they put bull testicles on my car," she said. "Now, if they'd damaged my car, I would have thought that was different."

Despite the resistance she encountered, Grandin has transformed the beef industry. Half of all cows slaughtered in the U.S. are killed in plants that use her equipment. She has also consulted with game parks, veterinarians, stockyards, and zoos. Huge corporations like McDonalds have hired her to oversee the way they process cattle for their hamburgers. Grandin may be the only person on earth who has been praised by both Burger King and the People for the Ethical Treatment of Animals.

Grandin insists that animals have helped her as much as she has helped them. As she says, "The strongest feeling that I have today is one of intense calm and serenity as I handle cattle and feel them relax under my care."

Grandin lectures at Colorado State University, where she is a professor of animal science. She also gives countless talks that provide insight into the minds of people with autism.

10
Not Less

In the years since her teenage panic attacks, Grandin has learned to manage her autism. Antidepressant medicines help ease her anxiety. The world still overwhelms her sometimes. But by 2010, she felt like she could do without her squeeze machine. "It broke . . . and I never got around to fixing it," she said. "I'm into hugging people now."

Over the years, however, Grandin has designed better squeeze machines for others. One version of the machine is recommended by doctors to help calm people with autism and attention deficit hyperactivity disorder (ADHD).

Grandin spends much of her time touring the country, lecturing on autism and animal care. Despite her success, she lives simply. Her style of dress never changes. Each day, she wears jeans, boots, and a cowgirl shirt with a Western kerchief and a cow-shaped pin.

She has close friends, but she spends most of her evenings at home. She reads science fiction and watches *Star Trek*. She identifies with the half-alien Mr. Spock and the android Lieutenant Data. They both struggle to understand human emotions.

Romantic feelings seem strange to Grandin. She has chosen not to pursue a

The HBO movie *Temple Grandin* was made in 2010. In this scene, a young Temple Grandin studies a model airplane with her science teacher and mentor, William Carlock.

love relationship. "I am told by my non-autistic friends that relationships with other people are what most people live for. Whereas, I get very attached to my projects and to certain places," she said. "I get great satisfaction out of doing clever things with my mind."

In her speeches and writing, Grandin insists that people with autism are different from, but not less than, the rest of the population. She urges parents to follow her mother's lead and make sure their kids interact with mainstream kids. She encourages teaching computer skills early on as a means of communication. And she asks that people focus less on changing the behavior of kids with autism and more on helping them cope.

In 2010 Temple Grandin (left) appeared at the "Night of Too Many Stars," an event to raise money to educate kids with autism. Among the stars were Robin Williams (right), Chris Rock, Tina Fey, Jimmy Fallon, and Jon Stewart. "I can't emphasize enough the importance of little kids' early educational intervention," Grandin said.

Mostly, she asks society to respect the remarkable feats that autistic people can achieve. "We've got to have a lot more emphasis on the talent," she says, "and not so much emphasis on the disability."

That is exactly the way she has come to view her own condition. Her peculiar way of thinking, she believes, has given her a unique understanding of people, animals, and science. "If I could snap my fingers and become non-autistic, I would not," she says, "because then I wouldn't be me."

Aside from her work with livestock, Grandin has changed the way the world understands people with autism. As one teacher of autistic children says, "These things [my students] experience every day, people don't understand. And [Grandin] explains it in a way they can understand . . ."

According to Grandin, autism has helped her. "It's like a little bit of the autistic trait can give some advantages," she says. "I feel very strongly that if you got rid of all of the autistic [traits], you're not going to have any scientists. There'd be no computer people. You'd lose a lot of artists and musicians. There'd be a horrible price to pay."

Temple Grandin

Born:

August 29, 1947

Grew up:

Boston, Massachusetts

Life's work:

Animal rights and autism advocacy

Day job:

Professor, author, and livestock consultant

Website:

www.templegrandin.com

Author of:

Animals in Translation: Using the Mysteries of Autism to Decode Animal Behavior
Animals Make Us Human: Creating the Best Life for Animals
Thinking in Pictures: And Other Reports from My Life with Autism
The Way I See It: A Personal Look at Autism and Asperger's

Inventor of:

The "Squeeze Machine" and machinery for the humane treatment of cattle

She says:

"I don't know if people will ever be able to talk to animals the way Doctor Doolittle could, or whether animals will be able to talk back. Maybe science will have something to say about that. But I do know people can learn to "talk" to animals, and hear what animals have to say, better than they do now."

A Conversation with Author
Jack Maher

Q *What was your process for researching and writing this book?*

A My usual method is to begin by conducting lengthy interviews with each subject. Unfortunately neither Millan nor Grandin was available for an interview. That made my job harder, but not impossible. I read tons of articles and interviews. I scoured their websites and watched several episodes of Millan's *Dog Whisperer.*

Some of the most important resources were their books. The most useful were Millan's book *Cesar's Way* and Grandin's *Thinking in Pictures.*

Q *Are there any particularly interesting things you learned but weren't able to include in the book?*

A Millan has many funny stories about the dogs he's trained—and even more about their owners. In one case, a married couple chose to live apart because their dogs didn't get along. I also thought it was funny that he'll put hyper dogs on treadmills to burn off their excess energy.

Q *What similarities do you see between Cesar Millan's and Temple Grandin's paths to success?*

A Obviously both overcame huge obstacles. They faced intense challenges communicating with people but had a remarkable affinity to animals. It made me wonder: were they drawn to animals as a replacement for human companionship? I don't know. But Millan was a stranger in the U.S. And Grandin's autism could make her feel cut off from the rest of the world.

Q *What do you find inspiring about their stories?*

A No one could have predicted Millan's or Grandin's success. Millan was a penniless immigrant. He sneaked across the border from Mexico to California. For a while, he lived on the streets. That's not exactly a typical résumé for a TV star. Grandin's autism is incredibly challenging. Many people with autism spend their entire lives struggling to communicate with others. Grandin became a leader in two fields. The determination they both showed is amazing.

Q *How do you think Temple Grandin's autism has affected her identity?*

A Her life has been filled with challenges. As a child she was teased by other kids. For most of her life she could barely stand another person's embrace. So certainly autism has limited her in some ways. But she would also say that autism has opened doors for her. She calls her thought-process "thinking in pictures." And she says it has expanded her scientific creativity and helped her understand animals.

Q *What experiences were most important in leading Millan and Grandin to their life's work?*

A Both had important experiences on farms. Millan's early years on his grandfather's farm formed his character. That's where he made his connection with animals, particularly the packs of wild dogs that roamed his grandfather's fields. While other kids were playing soccer, Millan was learning how to communicate with animals.

For Grandin, the summer she spent on her aunt's ranch changed her life. In the cattle "squeeze chute," she first experienced relief from her anxiety. She also observed farm animals and, like Millan, sensed a connection with them.

Q *How did support from others help to fuel their success?*

A Millan credits a long list of people with helping him become the "Dog Whisperer." His grandfather taught him every animal-training lesson he knew. His mother believed in his wild ambition to become the world's greatest dog trainer. And actress Jada Pinkett Smith set him on a path to TV stardom.

Grandin, too, acknowledges that she's relied on many helping hands. Foremost, she says, is her mother, who had the remarkably difficult task of helping an autistic child find a foothold in what often seemed like an alien world.

Q *How would you say that Millan and Grandin helped to build capacity for others?*

A Both Millan and Grandin are committed to easing the suffering of animals and helping animals and people live together peacefully. Of course they go about it in different ways! Millan helps humans and dogs work out harmonious relationships. And Grandin urges humans to take responsibility for the well-being of the animals they may someday eat.

What to Read Next

Fiction

The Beef Princess of Practical County, Michelle Houts. (240 pages) *Twelve-year-old Libby learns the ups and downs of raising cattle on her family's ranch.*

The Curious Incident of the Dog in the Night-Time, Mark Haddon. (226 pages) *An autistic 15-year-old boy tries to solve the mystery surrounding a neighbor's dead dog.*

My Dog Skip, Willie Morris. (128 pages) *A boy and his dog have adventures in a small southern town.*

Julie of the Wolves, Jean Craighead George. (208 pages) *When a pack of wolves begins to accept a young Eskimo girl into their community, she must learn to think like a wolf.*

Rules, Cynthia Lord. (224 pages) *Catherine finds life with her autistic brother difficult, so she gives him rules to follow.*

Marcelo in the Real World, Francisco X. Stork. (320 pages) *Marcelo, a 17-year-old boy with autism, learns to navigate the world.*

Nonfiction

Born on a Blue Day: Inside the Extraordinary Mind of an Autistic Savant, Daniel Tammet. (240 pages) *Tammet has autism, and he can speak ten languages and multiply and divide huge numbers with the speed and accuracy of a computer.*

A Dog Named Slugger, Leigh Brill. (248 pages) *A woman tells the story of how a dog helped her cope with illness.*

Books

Animals in Translation: Using the Mysteries of Autism to Decode Animal Behavior, Temple Grandin and Catherine Johnson. (372 pages) *Grandin explains her work and her insights into the minds of animals.*

Cesar's Rules: Your Way to Train a Well-Behaved Dog, Cesar Millan with Melissa J. Peltier. (320 pages) *Millan describes how to communicate with your dog and shares methods for teaching your dog how to be a happy, well-behaved member of your household.*

It's Me or the Dog: How to Have the Perfect Pet, Victoria Stilwell. (224 pages) *Stilwell presents clear, friendly advice to help dog owners raise happy, healthy, and obedient pets.*

Films and Videos

Animals Are Beautiful People (1974). *This is a documentary about the interesting and amusing things that the animals of southern Africa get into.*

Temple Grandin (2010). *This HBO movie about the life of Temple Grandin stars Claire Danes in the title role.*

The Very Best of Dog Whisperer with Cesar Millan (2009). *This DVD is a collection of some of the best-loved episodes of Cesar Millan's television series* Dog Whisperer.

Websites

www.cesarsway.com
Cesar Millan's official website has tips, photos, stories, and more.

www.templegrandin.com
Temple Grandin's autism website has links to her livestock site.

Glossary

abstract (AB-strakt) *adjective* based on ideas rather than things

android (AN-droid) *noun* a robot built to look and act like a human

autism (AW-tis-uhm) *noun* a brain condition that may cause a person to have trouble communicating and forming relationships with others

blueprint (BLOO-print) *noun* a detailed plan for a structure or project

canine (KAY-nine) *noun* a dog

chute (SHOOT) *noun* a narrow passage

corral (kuh-RAL) *noun* a fenced-in area for holding livestock

coyote (kye-OH-tee) *noun* in this book, a person who guides someone who is illegally crossing a border

diagnosis (di-ag-NOH-sis) *noun* the identification of a disorder or disease

dominant (DOM-uh-nuhnt) *adjective* the most influential or powerful

epitome (ep-IT-uh-mee) *noun* a typical or ideal example of something

institution (in-stuh-TOO-shuhn) *noun* a place to care for the sick or the mentally ill

integrity (in-TEG-ruh-tee) *noun* the quality of being honest and having strong moral principles

livestock (LIVE-stok) *noun* farm animals kept for use or profit, especially for food

mangy (MAYN-jee) *adjective* having many worn or bare spots in the fur

onslaught (ON-slawt) *noun* a violent and powerful attack

pack-oriented (PAK OR-ee-uhn-tuhd) *adjective* having one's attention directed to the group that one is part of

panic attack (PAN-ik uh-TAK) *noun* a sudden episode of intense fear

rehabilitate (REE-hab-il-uh-tate) *verb* to restore or bring to a condition of health or useful activity

slaughterhouse (SLAW-tur-houss) *noun* a building where animals are killed for their meat

squeeze chute (SKWEEZ SHOOT) *noun* a chute that squeezes livestock to calm them; used to make vaccinating or branding easier

stimuli (STIM-yuh-lye) *noun* smells, sights, sounds, and tastes that make an impact on the senses

stockyard (STOK-yard) *noun* an enclosed area where livestock are kept before being shipped or slaughtered

unruly (uhn-ROO-lee) *adjective* hard to control

Metric Conversions

acres to hectares: 1 acre is about 0.4 hectares

miles to kilometers: 1 mi is about 1.6 km

pounds to kilograms: 1 lb is about 0.45 kg

Sources

ALPHA DOG

Be the Pack Leader: Use Cesar's Way to Transform Your Dog . . . and Your Life, Cesar Millan with Melissa Jo Peltier. New York: Harmon Books, 2007. (including quote on page 53)

"Cesar Millan." *Charlie Rose Show*, August 30, 2006. (including quotes on pages 44, 45)

"Cesar Millan: Dog's Best Friend," Lucy Cavendish. *Telegraph*, March 2, 2008. (including quotes on pages 23, 32, 33, 41)

"Cesar Millan: A Sage for the Canine Set," Mimi Avins. *Los Angeles Times*, October 18, 2004. (including quotes on pages 31, 32)

Cesar's Rules: Your Way to Train a Well-Behaved Dog, Cesar Millan with Melissa Jo Peltier. New York: Crown Archetype, 2010. (including quote on page 4)

CesarsWay.com Cesar Millan's official website. (including quote on page 18)

Cesar's Way: The Natural, Everyday Guide to Understanding and Correcting Common Dog Problems, Cesar Millan with Melissa Jo Peltier. New York: Harmony Books, 2006. (including quotes on pages 18, 52)

"The Dog Whisperer: Canine Therapy." *ABC Nightline*, July 28, 2006. (including quote on pages 18–19)

"The 'Dog Whisperer' Has a Gift with Canines—and Humans," Matthew Gilbert. *Boston Globe*, October 5, 2007. (including quote on page 50)

"Leader of the Pack," Alexis Chu. *People Weekly*, October 26, 2009. (including quote on page 48)

"Leader of the Pack," John Patterson. *Guardian*, April 30, 2009.

"Leader of the Pack," Deborah Solomon. *New York Times Magazine*, May 7, 2006. (including quote on page 42)

"The Man Behind the Whisper," Mary-Jo Dionne. *Modern Dog.* (including quotes on pages 22, 26, 29–30)

"The Pet Economy," Diane Brady and Christopher Palmeri. *Businessweek*, August 6, 2007.

"Whispering to Rottweilers, and to C.E.O.'s," Amy Wallace. *New York Times*, October 10, 2009. (including quotes on pages 16, 31–32, 35, 48)

BREAKING THROUGH

"'All God's Creatures' Woman Responds to Autism." *ABC News*, March 18, 1994. (including quote on page 59)

Animals in Translation: Using the Mysteries of Autism to Decode Animal Behavior, Temple Grandin. New York: Scribner, 2005. (including quotes on pages 73, 101)

An Anthropologist on Mars: Seven Paradoxical Tales, Oliver Sacks. New York: Knopf, 1995.

"Autism and My Sensory Based World," interview with Temple Grandin. SpeechPathology.com, January 17, 2011.

"Brilliant, but Different: How Autistic Woman Earned Fame," Dave Eisenstadter. *Monadnock Ledger-Transcript.* (including quote on page 70)

"A Conversation with Temple Grandin." NPR's *All Things Considered*, April 29, 2002. (including quotes on pages 77, 79, 88, 100)

"CSU Professor Temple Grandin Shares Insights, Tips." *Coloradoan*, March 4, 2011. (including quote on page 99)

"Drawing on Autistic License," Dan Glaister. *Guardian*, June 2, 2005. (including quote on page 90)

"Five Things Temple Grandin Knows for Sure," Jessica Winter. *O Magazine*, February 2010. (including quotes on pages 5, 75)

Grandin.com Dr. Temple Grandin's livestock website. (including quote on page 86)

"A Life Devoted to Animals." NPR's *Talk of the Nation*, January 27, 2010.

"Picture Thinking in Pictures," Elaine O'Connor. *Vancouver Province*, August 10, 2008. (including quote on page 98)

"Q&A with Temple Grandin: Thinking in Pictures Provides Insight into the World of Animals," Claudia Kawczynska. *Bark*, Winter 2004. (including quote on page 84)

"Temple Grandin, The Cow Whisperer," Heather Smith Thomas. WesternCowman.com. (including quote on page 98)

"Temple Grandin Discusses Similarities Between People with Autism and Animals." NPR's *Fresh Air*, February 5, 2010. (including quotes on pages 68, 69, 80, 81, 84–85)

"Temple Grandin Interview," Greenmuze staff. GreenMuze.com, July 29, 2009. (including quote on page 80)

"Temple Grandin on Temple Grandin," Claudia Wallis. *Time*, February 4, 2010. (including quote on page 93)

TempleGrandin.com Dr. Temple Grandin's official website.

Thinking in Pictures: And Other Reports from My Life with Autism, Temple Grandin. New York: Doubleday, 1995. (including quotes on pages 61, 91, 96)

Index